N O P Q
WE ARE NOT
OVARY-ACTING
R S T
U V W
X Y Z

RBG A to Z

Smith Street Books

INTRODUCTION

Her birth name was Joan, her family called her Kiki, many knew her as Notorious RBG, but officially she was Justice Ruth Bader Ginsburg. Born in 1933, during the Depression era, Joan became Ruth when there were too many other little girls called Joan in her class. Her new name stuck, and little Ruth went on an incredible life journey from suburban Brooklyn all the way to the bench of the Supreme Court of the United States.

Along the way she dined with presidents, rubbed shoulders with celebs and captured the hearts and minds of ordinary people, who were fascinated by the slight-yet-mighty justice with a penchant for doing push-ups well into her eighties.

From winning landmark gender discrimination cases to penning influential dissents (written nonconcurrences with the majority decision) that put Congress on notice, fighting for equality was the name of Ruth's game. And just as she made her mark on the legal world, she also became a pop-culture phenomenon.

A true renaissance woman, Ruth's talents extended beyond the legal realm. Sure, she crafted sizzling dissents, but she also performed cameos in operas, made appearances on late-night talk shows and even officiated weddings.

Whether you remember her as a feminist icon, liberal superhero, great thinker, champion of equality, super-fit senior, or all of the above, Ruth's life was a masterclass in overcoming the odds. Navigating serious illness, personal loss, death threats, discrimination, and more to rise to the very top of her profession, Ruth was an unstoppable force of nature who changed the world for the better.

JO STEWART

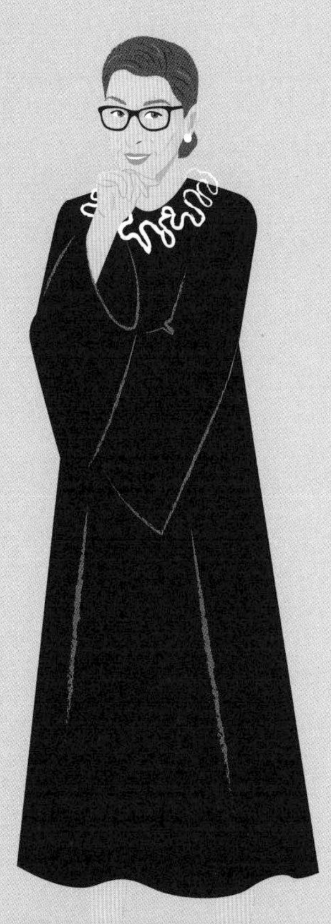

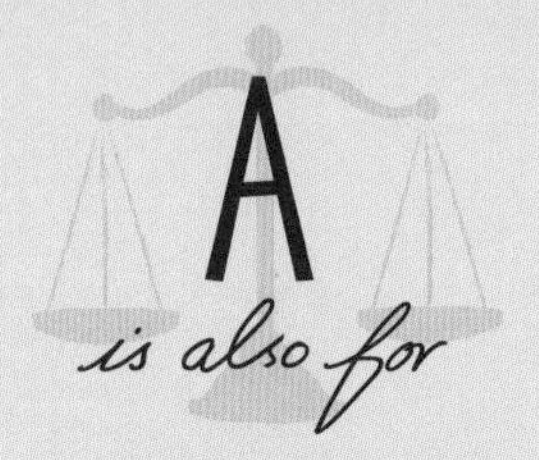

Awards

From the National Constitution Center's prestigious Liberty Medal to Harvard's esteemed Radcliffe Medal and the million-dollar Berggruen Prize, numerous awards were bestowed upon Ruth for her contributions to gender equality. Unsurprisingly, she channeled her million-dollar payday from the Berggruen Prize not towards buying a fleet of new Lamborghinis, but towards her favorite charitable organizations.

...

Ambition

Ambition wasn't exactly seen as a positive trait for women when Ruth was young. Regardless, Ruth was clear about her ambition from the get-go, with her college grades signaling she was a woman on a mission to forge a career in law. Even though she graduated equal first in her class at Columbia Law School, Ruth had trouble landing a job at a law firm, presumably due to her status as a wife and mother. Did this quell her ambition? Nope. Instead, it fueled her commitment to fighting gender discrimination and perhaps put her on a more ambitious career path than she'd considered before.

...

Josef Albers

Ruth and her husband Marty were art lovers, united in their admiration of painter Josef Albers' abstract prints and paintings. As a young couple, they fell in love with the work of the influential German-born artist, but, unable to afford any of his original works, they first borrowed a work from MoMA then settled for a reproduction from the museum gift shop. Years later, after decades of working her way up to the role of Supreme Court justice, Ruth was able to decorate her office with original art of her choosing, including two oil paintings by Albers.

The ACLU is supported by many celebrity ambassadors, including singer Cyndi Lauper, *Modern Family* actor Jesse Tyler Ferguson and veteran musician and activist Harry Belafonte.

Ruth's time at the ACLU concluded after she was appointed to the US Court of Appeals for the District of Columbia in 1980 – a huge step in her journey towards becoming a Supreme Court justice in later years.

Ever the overachiever, in the same year that Ruth began serving as ACLU's Women's Rights Project director, she also became Columbia Law School's first female tenured professor.

Although she was a champion of women's rights, some of Ruth's ACLU cases involved discrimination against men. Ruth believed that one of the best ways to convince judges of the realities of gender discrimination was to highlight that both men and women can be impacted by it.

For more than 100 years the American Civil Liberties Union (ACLU) has championed the rights of Americans. From defending reproductive rights to taking a stand for free speech and demanding the LGBTQI+ community receive equal treatment in the eyes of the law, the ACLU has fought many significant legal battles in the name of equality. Obviously, this trailblazing organization was the perfect place for Ruth to channel her passion for gender equality at a critical time in America's history. After volunteering for the organization in the 1960s, Ruth became the founding director of the ACLU's Women's Rights Project in 1972. For close to a decade Ruth was involved in more than 30 cases brought before the Supreme Court of the United States by the ACLU, resulting in many laws being rewritten to forever change women's legal status for the better.

Just like Michael Jordan, Jerry Seinfeld and Jay-Z, Ruth Bader Ginsburg was born in Brooklyn. Known for having great pride in their borough, these New Yorkers consider themselves Brooklynites first and foremost. Ruth grew up in the Midwood neighborhood, an area that attracted migrant families seeking to build a new life. She attended Public School 238 and James Madison High School, worshipped at the East Midwood Jewish Center, and tagged along with her mother to the Brooklyn Public Library. Even though her studies and career took her to other parts of the country, Ruth never forgot her roots. As a true daughter of Brooklyn, she returned to her old school to inspire the borough's children to work hard and dream big, just like she did.

Ruth's childhood home on East 9th Street in Midwood is still standing and is currently occupied by a couple who have lived there for more than 45 years. To date, they have declined many offers to sell the home.

Brooklyn is home to a bronze statue of Ruth that forms a part of the Statues for Equality series. Created by Australian artists Gillie and Marc, the statue concept was approved by Ruth before her death and now lives in Downtown Brooklyn's City Point building.

RUTH BADER GINSBURG

The high school Ruth attended in Brooklyn now runs a law program and even has a mock courtroom dedicated to her.

Her high school was also attended by many influential alumni, including Senator Bernie Sanders and another famous, fearless justice, Judge Judy Sheindlin.

In 2021, the Brooklyn Municipal Building was officially renamed the Justice Ruth Bader Ginsburg Brooklyn Municipal Building to honor the fearless woman who made an indelible mark on not just the nation, but the world.

B is also for

Bush v. Gore

Presidential elections don't get much more controversial than what went down in 2000 between Republican George 'Dubya' Bush and Democrat Al Gore. With the election result down to the wire, a recount was ordered in the state of Florida. That was until the US Supreme Court agreed to the Bush campaign's request for the recount to be halted, ultimately handing Bush the presidency. Justice Ginsburg was having none of it, and offered a strong dissenting opinion to the highly contentious ruling.

...

Burwell v. Hobby Lobby

One of Ruth's most famous dissents occurred during the *Burwell v. Hobby Lobby* case of 2014. When the Supreme Court's 5–4 decision effectively gave companies the right to deny women employees access to medical coverage for contraceptives such as IUDs, Ruth penned a blistering 35-page dissent against the majority opinion.

...

Blue

Considered to be the color of justice, blue lit up many landmarks across the state of New York to honor Ruth after she passed away, from the Grand Central Terminal in Manhattan to the New York State Education Building in Albany. It was a fitting and moving tribute to the diminutive woman from Brooklyn who fought for justice for so many.

Classical music

As a lifelong fan of classical music, it's unsurprising that Ruth's son, Jim, left law school to start a classical music label called Cedille Records. This label went on to release the *Notorious RBG in Song* album, a fitting musical tribute to Ruth's incredible life and legacy.

...

Constitution

While some people believe the Constitution should never be changed or updated, Ruth believed that a document created more than 200 years ago needed to adapt to the times. By believing in what's known as a "living constitution," Ruth recognized that word meanings change over time, as does the world we live in. Ruth also drew inspiration from other nations' constitutions. South Africa's constitution was one she often cited as being a worthy model for other countries to follow, as do many other legal scholars, who believe its focus on human rights and governance make it a shining example of a modern constitution.

...

Chutzpah

A Yiddish word derived from Hebrew, "chutzpah" is a word meaning courage or audacity. The Merriam-Webster dictionary defines it as "supreme self-confidence." When considering what courage and confidence it took for a young Jewish woman from Brooklyn to study at Ivy League colleges, stare down the US Supreme Court while fighting gender discrimination cases, and then join the Supreme Court as a jurist and write epic dissents that have gone down in history, it becomes very clear that Ruth had chutzpah in spades.

Ruth was a member of Phi Beta Kappa, a prestigious academic honor society that's existed since 1776.

While studying at Cornell University, Ruth belonged to the Alpha Epsilon Phi sorority.

While working at Rutgers University in the 1960s, Ruth was told she was paid less than male professors because they had families to support. Five female professors working at the college launched an equal pay suit, which was settled in 1969.

When Harvard bestowed on Ruth an honorary law degree in 2011, Spanish opera singer Plàcido Domingo (a fellow honorary degree recipient) sang for her during the conferral, much to Ruth's delight.

C *is for* COLLEGE

Education was of huge importance to Ruth – this was instilled in her by her progressive mother, Celia. Ruth ended up studying at three prestigious Ivy League schools – an astonishing achievement for a woman born in the 1930s. Straight after high school, Ruth completed a bachelor's degree in Government from Cornell University's College of Arts and Sciences (leaving with top marks, of course). Next was Harvard Law School, where she was one of just nine women in a class of more than 500 men. In her third year of study, she moved back to New York due to her husband, Marty, receiving a job opportunity, completing her law degree at Columbia Law School and tying for first in the class. Despite being a superior scholar with strong recommendations from professors, Ruth struggled to find work after graduation, being knocked back from clerkships due to her gender. Later she became a professor at Rutgers and Columbia Law Schools, where she shaped the next generation of lawyers, in the case of the latter giving back to the college that kickstarted her blockbuster career.

SANDRA *is for* DAY O'CONNOR

While Ruth Bader Ginsburg smashed a fair few glass ceilings in her time, it was Sandra Day O'Connor who rose to become the first woman to serve on the Supreme Court of the United States – not bad for someone who grew up on a remote cattle ranch in Arizona without electricity or running water. For 12 long years, Sandra served as the sole woman on the US Supreme Court, until Ruth joined her as the second woman to claim the pinnacle of judicial power. As a pragmatic conservative, it would appear that someone like Sandra wouldn't have much in common with a liberal like Ruth. Yet it was their shared experiences of being underestimated that united them. Both Ruth and Sandra had trouble securing employment in law firms after graduating, and both overcame huge obstacles to claim the most senior and influential role in their profession. Over the years they enjoyed a chalk and cheese–style connection based on mutual respect and admiration, even though their backgrounds, cultures, religions and political persuasions were poles apart. As women who both had the intelligence, gravitas and know-how to navigate the male-dominated legal world, let's clock up Ruth and Sandra's friendship to game recognizing game.

In 2009, then president Barack Obama awarded Sandra Day O'Connor the Presidential Medal of Freedom, the highest honor a United States civilian can be given.

Sandra wrote several books, including children's books *Chico* (2005) and *Finding Susie* (2009), both based on her childhood experiences growing up on a ranch in the desert.

In 2019, Ruth Bader Ginsburg and Sandra Day O'Connor's relationship was depicted in *Sisters in Law*, a spirited stage show based on the bestselling book.

American lawyer and author Linda Hirshman penned *Sisters in Law: How Sandra Day O'Connor and Ruth Bader Ginsburg Went to the Supreme Court and Changed the World*, an in-depth book detailing Sandra's and Ruth's parallel journeys and lasting legacies.

D *is also for*

Discrimination

Fighting discrimination in all its forms was what Ruth was all about. While known for her contributions towards ending gender discrimination, she also fought to end discrimination based on race, ethnicity, sexual orientation, and religious beliefs.

...

Deli

As a child, Ruth was influenced by many strong women, but it was the women of Russ & Daughters deli that made a lasting impact. As the first business in the country to be named "& Daughters" (instead of "& Sons"), the now-famous, originally Lower East Side Jewish deli did more than just provide Ruth and her family with bagels and lox. The popular eatery also inadvertently shaped the mind of a future Supreme Court justice by showing her that women can be business owners – a huge revelation for a young girl in the 1930s and 1940s.

...

Documentary

Released in 2018, the documentary *RBG* was partly responsible for accelerating Ruth's fame outside of America. Directed by Julie Cohen and Betsy West, the inspiring film took viewers on a revelatory, behind-the-scenes journey into Ruth's extraordinary life. Earning BAFTA and Oscar nominations for best documentary, and winning a primetime Emmy, the popular film was well received by both critics and the public, and it became one of the highest-grossing indie films of the year. Sure, Ruth was a formidable legal scholar, but she had box-office pulling power too!

E is also for

Editor
As the former editor of the *Columbia Law Review* and known for her persuasive writing skills, Ruth had exceptionally high standards when it came to the written word. Clerks who served with her over the years will attest to Ruth's savage editing skills, with bench memos often being returned to clerks covered in red ink. As a precise writer and sharp communicator, Ruth ultimately coached her clerks to become better writers themselves, after they'd recovered from seeing their work obliterated by a five-foot octogenarian armed with a red pen.

...

Equal Credit Opportunity Act
In the early 1970s, Ruth worked on many cases that highlighted examples of how men and women were treated differently by financial institutions, including a key case that challenged a state law that deemed men to be the preferred administrators of an estate. This case (along with many others) contributed to a growing consensus that the status quo had to change and led to the creation of the *Equal Credit Opportunity Act*, which made it illegal for financial institutions to discriminate against any applicant based on their gender, race, religion, marital status, or age.

...

Empowerment
A woman who was unafraid to lead with strength and integrity, Ruth emboldened generations of women to step into their power. From changing laws to allow women to enroll in previously male-only colleges, to helping to stop pregnancy-related discrimination in the workplace, Ruth had a hand in empowering women to occupy courtrooms, board meetings, military positions, prestigious educational institutions, and anywhere else they'd been denied entry to for centuries.

Ruth not only advocated for gender equality in workplaces and in the eyes of the law – she also believed in equality in the home, saying, "Women will have achieved true equality when men share with them the responsibility of bringing up the next generation."

In the 1970s, Ruth won five pivotal US Supreme Court cases based on the Equal Protection Clause of the Constitution's 14th Amendment. These cases highlighted that the amendment didn't only apply to racial equality, but gender equality also.

We the People

Article 1

In a 1973 Supreme Court case seeking greater gender equality within US Air Force policies, Ruth quoted nineteenth-century women's rights activist Sarah Moore Grimké: "I ask no favors for my sex … All I ask of our brethren is, that they will take their feet from off our necks."

E is for EQUALITY

The notion of equality was something Ruth grappled with from a young age, when she noticed women were excluded from Jewish rituals she wished to take part in. Yet when it came to championing equality, Ruth played the long game. She knew that unpicking centuries of entrenched systemic inequality would take time and required sharp, succinct arguments. Fortunately, Ruth was both a persuasive writer and a pro at building strong legal cases. She also had time (mostly) on her side, enjoying a legal career that spanned more than five decades, including 27 highly influential years on the US Supreme Court bench. She first emerged as a champion for equality in the 1970s, when she argued in the Supreme Court that women were entitled to equal rights under the law. It was these cases that laid the foundation for women to receive equal standing in workplaces and society. Once a victim of inequality, then a powerful advocate for equal opportunity, Ruth was dedicated to the pursuit of equality across her whole life.

The Atlantic labeled her a "feminist gladiator", *Harper's Bazaar* called her a "feminist hero," and *Forbes* named her a "feminist rock star" – Ruth was a feminist icon through and through. From battling workplace discrimination as a working mother to winning cases left, right and center as an ACLU Women's Rights Project litigator, Ruth advanced through life with a strong sense that women should not be held back, treated differently, discriminated against, or deemed lesser than men. While many people wrongly associate feminism with radical firebrands hell-bent on getting revenge on men, Ruth knew that change was possible without the fireworks. Preferring slow, precise, considered, incremental change, Ruth's brand of feminism was of the "silent but deadly" variety. Having experienced gender discrimination at many points in her life, Ruth fought the good feminist fight not on the streets, but in the courtroom.

Ruth belonged to what's known as "second wave feminism", a movement that began in the early 1960s and focussed on reproductive rights, sexuality, workplace discrimination, and gender roles within the home.

As a teenager, Ruth's feminist mother, Celia, marched in suffragette parades in New York, in support of women being granted the right to vote.

Pioneering feminist organizer Gloria Steinem said in 2020: "Ruth is a great instructor in bravery because she was a movement before there was a movement."

Ruth Bader Ginsburg–themed placards were prevalent at the Women's March protests held nationwide from 2017. One placard said VOTE (T)RUTH.

Fighter

Staring down cancer multiple times is not exactly something you'd wish for in life, but Ruth was up to the task. Just as Ruth fought for equality, she was also a tremendous combatant when it came to illness. After first being diagnosed with colon cancer in 1999, Ruth went on to fight lung and pancreatic cancer. Even as treatment took a toll on her body, she continued to plow through work, pull off speaking engagements and attend events. While Ruth blazed a trail in the courts, her fighting spirit showed the world that people living with cancer can achieve so very much.

...

Fame

From appearing on late-night talk shows to pulling off cameos in operas and becoming the focus of a Hollywood movie and indie documentary, Ruth's fame accelerated in the final years of her life. Instead of letting fame change or bother her, the octogenarian took this newfound celebrity status in her stride. Until the end she remained the same humble, gracious, grounded, and accessible person she was throughout her entire life.

...

Farewell

Aside from Ruth's private funeral and public memorial, many people chose to farewell her in their own special way with candlelight vigils. Many people also honored Ruth's legacy with a cash donation. Democratic candidates and progressive not-for-profits reported a huge upswell in donations following her passing, with more than $90 million reportedly given to Democratic candidates and causes in the 28 hours after Ruth's death – a record-breaking surge in donations. For many ordinary people, the best way to farewell her was to put their money towards organizations that were fighting the same fight Ruth did for most of her life.

Gloves
Just like Mickey Mouse, mime artist Marcel Marceau, and Madonna in the 1980s, Ruth loved rocking gloves. She began to curate a large collection of gloves in the late 1990s, when she first started wearing them to protect her hands during cancer treatment. She liked gloves so much she kept wearing them even after her treatment ended. From black fish-net gloves to delicate embroidered numbers, Ruth wore her hand accessories in court, at events, and even on the cover of *Time* magazine.

...

Grave
Ruth's grave can be found at Arlington National Cemetery in the state of Virginia; she is buried next to her husband, Marty. The historic military cemetery is home to veterans of many wars, dating all the way back to the American Civil War. While neither Ruth nor Marty served in a war, Marty did serve in the Army Reserve. Regardless, US Supreme Court justices and their spouses can be laid to rest at Arlington Cemetery, which is only ten minutes from Washington, DC.

...

Groundbreaking
Most of us mere mortals have hobbies to occupy our time, but for Ruth, breaking new ground was one of her favorite things to do. Over her life, she chalked up an impressive collection of 'firsts'. In college, she became the first female member of the highly regarded *Harvard Law Review*. In the 1990s she became the first Jewish woman to serve as a justice at the Supreme Court of the United States. And when she passed away, she became the first woman to lie in state at the US Capitol building. Even death couldn't stop Ruth from breaking new ground.

In the 1970s, a widower was refused social security benefits after his wife passed away during childbirth. Ruth argued that the *Social Security Act* was discriminatory. Ruth's victory in court ensured that both widowed men's rights were secured, and women's work was valued.

Ruth worked to overturn a statute in Florida that exempted women from appearing on the jury list. If women wanted to serve on a jury, they needed to apply, unlike men, who were automatically added to the jury duty list once they became adults.

During an interview with *USA Today*, Ruth was quoted as saying: "Women belong in all places where decisions are being made. It shouldn't be that women are the exception."

When Ruth attended Harvard, women weren't allowed in the college library. Women guests were not invited to the *Harvard Law Review* banquet, and were not given space in the Law School dormitories.

G *is for* GENDER EQUALITY

As someone who faced the sting of gender inequality in her own life, Ruth understood the pain of being discriminated against. While she presented and presided over many cases during her epic career, it was her contributions towards gender discrimination cases that she'll probably be best remembered for. While women were out marching for equality in the 1970s, Ruth was pushing for change the best way she knew how: within the courts. Working on pivotal cases that overturned statutes and rewrote laws for the better, Ruth destroyed centuries of entrenched gender inequality. And she was super smart about it, too. Instead of just taking on cases that highlighted discrimination against women, Ruth was known for leading cases that impacted men. From helping single fathers secure social security benefits to ensuring men, too, could be viewed as carers for dependants, Ruth demonstrated that parenting and caregiving weren't just the domain of women. This clever approach to highlighting sex-based discrimination became a hallmark of Ruth's career as a lawyer and put an end to women (and women's work) being viewed as inferior in the eyes of the law.

In 2002, Ruth was inducted into the National Women's Hall of Fame, an organization that honors women's contributions to the nation. She now occupies a place in the hall alongside a collection of other powerful, influential women, including her friend and fellow Supreme Court colleague Sandra Day O'Connor. So far, almost 300 women have been inducted into the Hall of Fame for achievements in politics, arts, sports, science, human rights, and beyond. Ruth travelled from DC to Seneca Falls to deliver her induction speech, despite it being only a few days before the first Monday in October – the day the US Supreme Court reconvenes after the summer break. In her induction speech, she said she found the invitation to attend her induction into the National Women's Hall of Fame "impossible to resist."

The National Women's Hall of Fame is in Seneca Falls, New York – the site of the first women's rights convention in the US in 1848.

Author Maya Angelou, media mogul Oprah Winfrey, pioneering aviator Amelia Earhart, and celebrated activist Rosa Parks are all also honored in the National Women's Hall of Fame.

Founded in 1969, the National Women's Hall of Fame is now housed in a building that was once a knitting mill – textiles being an industry renowned for employing women.

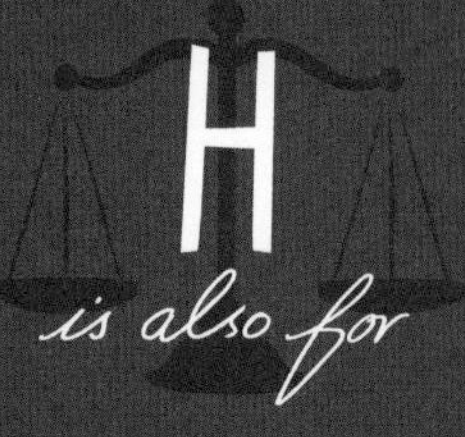

Health

Throughout her life, Ruth faced many health battles, yet she managed to bounce back time and time again. When news of her death broke in September 2020, many people were genuinely shocked that the 87-year-old dynamo had finally succumbed to cancer. Given her track record at kicking illness to the curb, the world collectively assumed she'd rise again to resume her place in the Supreme Court. In her later years, Ruth had triumphed over multiple cancer battles, emergency gall-bladder treatment, a nasty fall resulting in fractured ribs, and heart surgery following chest pains, but she took each health setback in her stride, until she could go on no more.

...

Height

Although Ruth was a giant in the eyes of many, she was a diminutive woman, reported to be only 5 feet 1 inch in height. Despite being short statured and slight, Ruth's supersized intellect, killer work ethic and self-assured persona enabled her to reach metaphorical heights.

...

Hot dogs

Although Ruth presided over many landmark legal judgments, she also handed down an important ruling in an episode of *The Late Show with Stephen Colbert*. After some careful questioning and deep thought, she confirmed that hot dogs are indeed sandwiches – thus ending a long-running debate about one of America's favorite eats.

Idols

When Ruth was asked who she idolized as a child, she said her mother, Celia, and one-time first lady Eleanor Roosevelt; the latter, interestingly, rose to that position the year Ruth was born. Roosevelt was also a United Nations diplomat and humanitarian, advocating for the expansion of women's roles in the workplace and for civil rights for African Americans and Asian Americans. From 1936 to 1962, Roosevelt wrote a regular newspaper column, which Celia would read aloud to her daughter. The benefits of reading to children are well known, but in this case, Celia's efforts to educate her daughter had a profound impact beyond expanding her vocabulary.

...

Irreplaceable

Even though Ruth was replaced on the US Supreme Court bench, her sharp intellect, indomitable spirit, and quirks have made her fundamentally irreplaceable – both within the Supreme Court and in the wider world.

...

Ilomantis ginsburgae

Ruth's influence on the legal sector is well known, but she also left her mark on the world of natural science when a new species of praying mantis was named after her in 2016. Found in Madagascar, *Ilomantis ginsburgae* is the first praying mantis species characterized by its female genitalia, instead of the male genitalia that's historically been used to classify insect species. Named in honor of Ruth, the species was identified after a study conducted by the Cleveland Museum of Natural History – led by a woman, of course.

Whenever Ruth was about to rip out a dissenting opinion, she'd wear her decorative dissent collar. Following her death, Banana Republic reissued a special edition of the famous dissent collar, with all proceeds donated to the International Center for Research on Women.

While it's customary for Supreme Court judges to use the phrase "I respectfully dissent" Ruth took a sword to tradition by omitting "respectfully" from her dissent in the *Bush v. Gore* case.

Ruth wrote her final dissenting opinion in July 2020, when she opposed proposed changes to laws that would allow more employers to opt out of providing medical coverage for contraceptives to women.

In 2014, YouTube–famous singer-songwriter Jonathan Mann turned one of Ruth's more fiery dissents into a song called "Ginsburg's Hobby Lobby Dissent".

I DISSENT

I *is for* I DISSENT

Although all Supreme Court justices provide dissenting opinions at one time or another, Ruth's dissents were the stuff of legend. With a dissent acting as a "path marker" (one of Ruth's favorite terms) to a different, imagined future, Ruth took the act of dissenting seriously. While she may not have been able to secure the result she wanted for all the cases she presided over in the Supreme Court, writing – or saying – "I dissent" enabled her to offer an alternative viewpoint to the majority opinion. Although dissents are usually presented in written form, Ruth broke with tradition and read hers aloud during the *Ledbetter v. Goodyear Tire & Rubber Co.* case of 2007. Her decision to verbalize this particular dissent demonstrated how strongly she felt about the need to deal with the gender pay gap. As a result of this strong dissent, the salary inequalities that exist between men and women was put on the national agenda, with Congress ultimately introducing the *Lilly Ledbetter Fair Pay Act* two years later.

J *is for* BRYANT JOHNSON

SUPER DIVA

Supreme Court justices aren't exactly known for their physical prowess, but thanks to Ruth's relationship with personal trainer Bryant Johnson, RBG became a senior fitness influencer. Ruth buddied up with Bryant back in 1999, around the time her health had taken a battering due to cancer treatment. But he soon turned that around by putting Ruth through her paces twice a week in the Supreme Court gym (yes, there's a gym hidden away behind those imposing stone walls). Not one to shrink from a challenge, Ruth went into full beast mode in the gym. She shredded her way into shape by following Bryant's demanding regime of cardio and resistance training. From performing push-ups and planks to working up a sweat on the elliptical trainer and bench pressing like a boss, Ruth's epic workouts kept her fit, focussed and feeling the burn right into her late eighties. The man credited with keeping the justice in shape for decades honored her by performing three poignant push-ups beside her coffin when she lay in state at the US Capitol – a fitting tribute from one gym rat to another.

Bryant Johnson penned *The RBG Workout*, an illustrated book that empowers anyone to shred like Ruth with a no-nonsense routine that can be done at home without gym equipment.

Bryant often referred to Ruth as T.A.N., which stands for "tough as nails."

Bryant served in the military for three decades, with 12 years spent in the United States Army Special Operations Command (Airborne).

Ruth and Bryant featured on an episode of *The Late Show with Stephen Colbert*, where the host joined the duo in the gym for a workout.

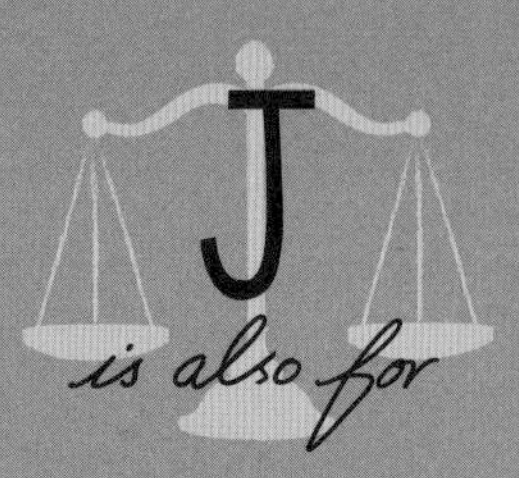

Jabots

Ruth's penchant for wearing decorative collars (also known as jabots) with her judicial robes made her an accidental fashion icon. From delicate white lace jabots to chunky golden collars, Ruth's range of neck accessories was watched closely by pundits after she revealed she matched her collars to each occasion. Naming a metallic neckpiece her "dissenting collar," Ruth made sure everyone in the chamber knew what was coming when she walked in wearing the symbolic metal suit of armor.

...

Justice

Ruth first became Justice Ginsburg in 1980 when she was appointed to the US Court of Appeals District of Columbia, but the word "justice" meant something to her long before that. The pursuit of justice was something she followed keenly from childhood, even writing an article on the Charter of the United Nations for her school newspaper when she was a young teen. Noticing injustices in the world as a youngster set Ruth up for a lifetime working in the judicial system.

...

Judaism

Ruth grew up in an observant Jewish family, so her faith and identity were important to her from the very beginning, even though Ruth was perplexed by the gender inequality entrenched in the belief system. It was Judaism's commitment to justice that led her to become interested in the law and how it's applied in America. Being part of a minority community with a long history of being discriminated against also shaped Ruth's views on equality. When she was named as the first Jewish woman to serve on the US Supreme Court, Ruth's dream of committing her life to the pursuit of justice – guided by her cultural identity – was fulfilled yet again.

Kiki

Bestowed on Ruth by her older sister, Kiki was the name by which Ruth was known to her close family and friends. The sweet nickname apparently came about due to Ruth kicking a lot as a baby.

...

Kin

Ruth and Marty had two children: Jane and James. Naturally, both are high achievers, enjoying careers that mirror their influential mother's talents and interests. Jane decided to follow in Ruth's footsteps and is now a law professor and attorney. Her son, James, also attended law school, but traded it in to follow another of his mother's passions by running a classical music record label. But Ruth's influence doesn't end there. Her granddaughter is a legal fellow with the ACLU, which would surely bring a smile to Ruth's face.

...

Knowledge

Known for having a strong memory and a sharp mind well into her senior years, Ruth was a great collector and keeper of knowledge. As a legal scholar, she'd stay up well into the early hours of morning to study and read as much as she could. But beyond the world of law, Ruth just loved learning. She cultivated a wealth of knowledge on everything from operatic history to the great painters of the contemporary art world, leading her to become known as one of the great thinkers of the century.

The John F. Kennedy Center for the Performing Arts officially opened in 1971 and is described as a "living memorial" to the US president who was known as a great supporter of arts and culture.

Following Ruth's death, the Washington National Opera performed a tribute concert featuring excerpts from Ruth's favorite operas, held at the Kennedy Center Opera House.

When attending opera performances at the Kennedy Center Opera House, Ruth preferred to enter quietly from a side door. During some of the last performances she attended, audiences gave her a huge round of applause and even a standing ovation.

is for

KENNEDY CENTER

Living only a hop, skip and a jump away from the John F. Kennedy Center for the Performing Arts meant that Ruth treated this iconic DC institution a bit like a second home. She was a regular in the audience of many performances, especially after her beloved husband, Marty, passed away. Hosting more than 2000 shows and events each year, the center offered plenty of options for Ruth to choose from. She also regularly took to its stage, captivating audiences with everything from fun opera cameos to in-depth talks on topics like arts and the law. She even officiated a wedding at the Kennedy Center. When news broke that Ruth had passed away, Kennedy Center staff were devastated, with many claiming that the building isn't the same without Ruth's sparkling presence.

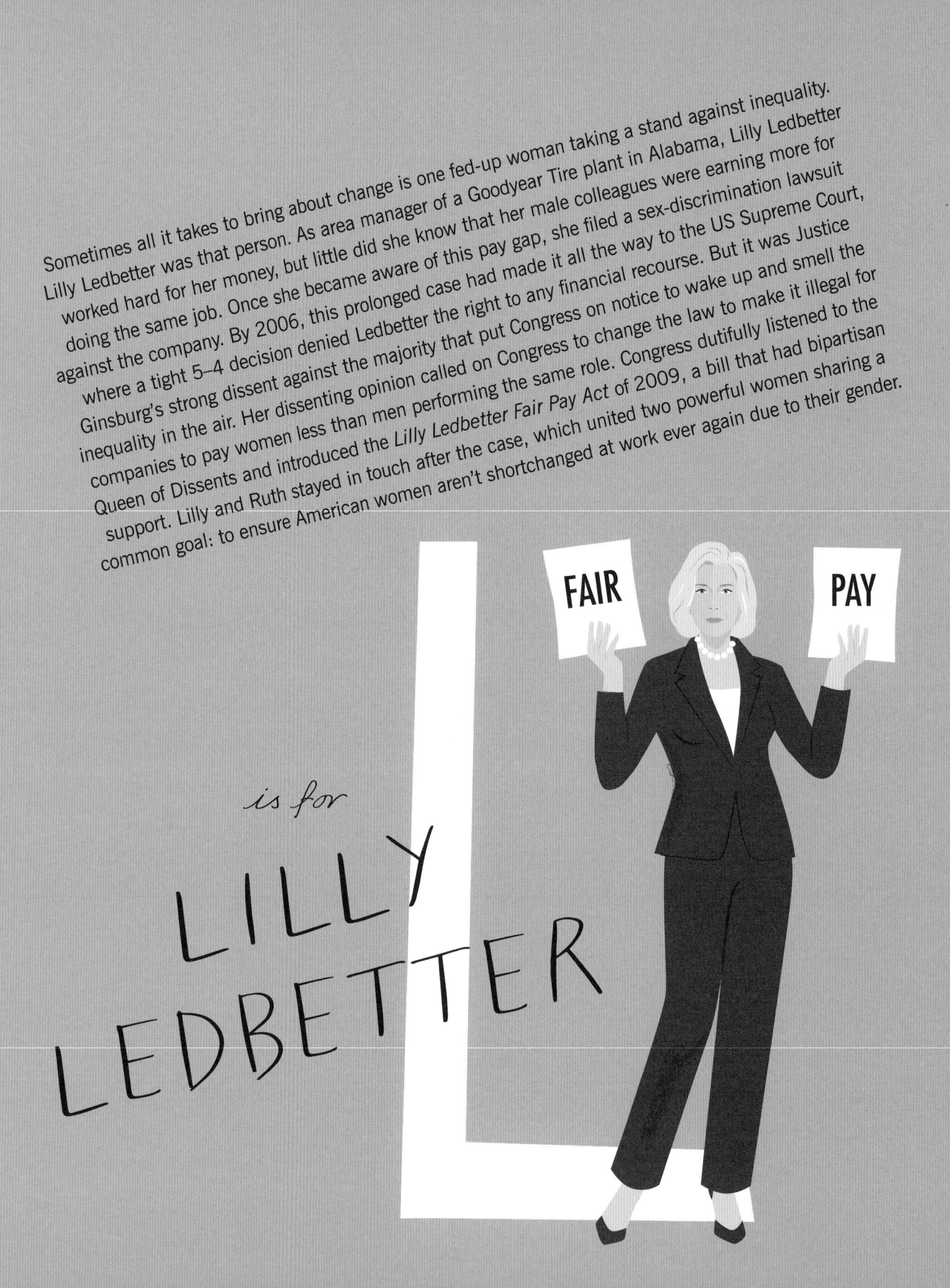

L is for LILLY LEDBETTER

Sometimes all it takes to bring about change is one fed-up woman taking a stand against inequality. Lilly Ledbetter was that person. As area manager of a Goodyear Tire plant in Alabama, Lilly Ledbetter worked hard for her money, but little did she know that her male colleagues were earning more for doing the same job. Once she became aware of this pay gap, she filed a sex-discrimination lawsuit against the company. By 2006, this prolonged case had made it all the way to the US Supreme Court, where a tight 5–4 decision denied Ledbetter the right to any financial recourse. But it was Justice Ginsburg's strong dissent against the majority that put Congress on notice to wake up and smell the inequality in the air. Her dissenting opinion called on Congress to change the law to make it illegal for companies to pay women less than men performing the same role. Congress dutifully listened to the Queen of Dissents and introduced the *Lilly Ledbetter Fair Pay Act* of 2009, a bill that had bipartisan support. Lilly and Ruth stayed in touch after the case, which united two powerful women sharing a common goal: to ensure American women aren't shortchanged at work ever again due to their gender.

After Ruth's passing, Lilly Ledbetter told *NBC News* that Ruth "changed my life, and she changed the country."

EQUAL PAY FOR EQUAL WORK

Ruth had a framed copy of the *Lilly Ledbetter Fair Pay Act* hanging in her office at the Supreme Court.

PUBLIC LAW 111-2-JAN. 29, 2009 123 STAT.5

Public Law 111-2
111th Congress

An Act

SECTION 1. SHORT TITLE

This Act may be cited as the "Lilly Ledbetter Fair Pay Act of 2009"

SEC.2 FINDINGS.

Despite the fact that during the trial he was battling cancer, Lilly Ledbetter's husband turned up regularly to court to support his wife. Unfortunately he passed away before seeing the introduction of the *Lilly Ledbetter Fair Pay Act*.

Barack Obama signed the Lilly Ledbetter bill into law in January 2009. It was the first bill he signed into law during his presidency.

Legacy

When people in the public eye pass away, the word "legacy" is thrown around a lot, but in the case of Ruth Bader Ginsburg, her legacy is truly immense. From contributing to monumental legal amendments to inspiring generations of women to study law, Ruth's legacy is both deep and multifaceted. Because of Ruth we live in a more equal society, more women are empowered to take charge of their lives, and we all have a new benchmark for what we expect from Supreme Court justices. Sure, we expect them to ensure everyone receives equal justice under law, but we'd also like a side serve of relatable content for the meme generation. It's what Ruth would have wanted.

...

Left-handed

Like former presidents Barack Obama, Bill Clinton and Ronald Reagan, Ruth was left-handed. As a child, she was once forced to write with her right hand, but after receiving a D for her efforts, she refused to ever write with her right hand again. Being a southpaw is associated with processing information differently and taking a more novel (potentially less logical) approach to problem solving. Either way, being a leftie in a right-handed person's world clearly didn't hold Ruth back one iota.

...

Ladder

At first, Ruth found it hard to get a foothold on the corporate ladder as a young, married, pregnant woman attempting to enter a male-dominated profession. But once she got her foot on the bottom rung, she ascended to the very top of the ladder, outshining most (if not all) of her male peers, who never reached the dizzying heights that she managed to in spite of rampant gender discrimination.

M *is also for*

Marginalized communities
Supporting women, migrants, minorities, and the LGBTQI+ community was one of the main reasons Ruth got out of bed in the morning. Some say that this strong sense of purpose gave her longevity. Instead of sitting in a rocking chair doing crossword puzzles in her twilight years, Ruth was hell-bent on righting the wrongs of the world. She was once quoted as saying she wanted to help repair tears in society, and she did just that by supporting marginalized people in receiving equal treatment in the eyes of the law.

...

Memes
In her later years, Ruth became a bit of a meme queen. The meme-ification of a Supreme Court justice wasn't something America had seen before, but young people really ran with it, whipping up "You can't spell truth without Ruth" memes with gusto. Some say reducing such a giant of the legal world to a pithy meme dilutes her legacy; others point out that the tidal wave of Ruth memes that emerged in her final years helped to engage a whole new generation with the goings-on of the stuffy, staid US Supreme Court. Either way, Ruth memes are here to stay.

...

Pauli Murray
The work of activist Pauli Murray had a big influence on Ruth. A woman way ahead of her time, Pauli may be relatively unknown, but her fierce determination to call out discrimination against women, black people, and queer communities made her a giant within the activism scene of the 1960s. Both Pauli and Ruth worked at the ACLU, with Pauli laying the groundwork for Ruth to go on and fight gender discrimination cases in the US Supreme Court in the 1970s. Pauli's work was so important to Ruth, she put Pauli's name on the front page of the first women's rights brief she wrote – a true mark of respect.

Marty was remembered with a cookbook created in his honor. *Chef Supreme: Martin Ginsburg* highlights Marty's love of gastronomy and is sold in the Supreme Court gift shop.

Marty famously said to *The New York Times* in 1997: "As a general rule, my wife does not give me any advice about cooking, and I do not give her advice about the law. This seems to work quite well on both sides."

The American Bar Association featured some of Marty's recipes in the *Nineteenth Amendment Centennial Cookbook*, a book filled with recipes by lawyers, jurists, executives, and media figures, among others, and dedicated to celebrating 100 years since women were granted the right to vote in the US.

Marty was diagnosed with testicular cancer while studying at Harvard with Ruth in 1957. Ever the trooper, Ruth managed to care for Marty and their baby daughter while continuing to study at Harvard Law School during this difficult time.

M *is for* MARTY GINSBURG

They say that behind every great man is a great woman, but in the case of Ruth and Marty Ginsburg, the saying could be reversed. Married for more than 50 years, Marty and Ruth started dating while they were studying at Cornell, and they ended up setting the bar extremely high from the get-go. *The Notebook* has nothing on these two! While Marty was attracted to Ruth's beauty, it was her brain that he fell in love with. A generous, jovial tax attorney, Marty was Ruth's best friend and greatest supporter. For a man born in the 1930s he held incredibly progressive views. While many men of his vintage would feel insecure at having such a successful, high-profile wife, Marty championed Ruth's career and revelled in her success. He actively supported Ruth by taking on all the cooking himself, creating restaurant-quality dishes. Sadly, Marty passed away in 2010, leaving a heartfelt, adoring letter to Ruth written in the days before he died.

When NYU student Shana Knizhnik set up a Tumblr account dedicated to Ruth Bader Ginsburg, she couldn't have imagined the impact her idea would have. Dubbing Ruth "Notorious RBG" proved to be a masterstroke, as Justice Ginsburg (and her admirers) embraced her new nickname with glee. What started as a Tumblr account soon became a *New York Times* best-selling book and a full-scale cultural phenomenon. Playing on the stage name of legendary rapper Christopher George Latore Wallace (aka Biggie Smalls or the Notorious B.I.G.), Ruth's new nickname reflected her reputation for crafting dissenting opinions that raised eyebrows. Even though Biggie Smalls was killed in the late 1990s, the revered rapper's cultural influence is still strong. Although no one could have predicted that an elderly Supreme Court justice would be united in name with one of the biggest artists of the 1990s gangsta rap scene, their shared influence on pop culture lives on.

is for

NOTORIOUS RBG

After coining Notorious RBG in 2015, Shana Knizhnik went on to become a lawyer (just like Ruth) and worked at the American Civil Liberties Union (just like Ruth).

In an interview with NPR, Ruth admitted she had a large supply of Notorious RBG shirts, which she liked to gift to people.

Ruth was more than comfortable with sharing the "notorious" moniker with rapper Biggie Smalls, as they were both from Brooklyn. "It seems altogether natural," she said.

In her speech accepting an honorary degree from the University at Buffalo, Ruth said: "It was beyond my wildest imagination that I would one day become the 'Notorious RBG.'"

Vladimir Nabokov

So what has a Russian novelist born in the late 1800s got to do with a Supreme Court justice like Ruth Bader Ginsburg? Well, the author of *Lolita* taught European literature classes at Cornell University while Ruth was there. His influence on her was profound, with Ruth crediting Nabokov with changing the way she read and wrote. Even though he wasn't teaching legal writing, Ruth took Nabokov's instruction to heart and carried it with her throughout her career. Known for being an incisive, persuasive writer, Ruth went on to write speeches and books, and many convincing legal arguments that changed the course of American history.

...

New York

Even though Ruth spent much of her adult life living in DC, she was frequently in a New York state of mind. She'd often hop over to her home state to view opera performances, attend gallery openings, and sit in the audience of Broadway shows. As a culture vulture with a love for the performing arts, Ruth was a beloved figure in the New York arts scene and is greatly missed by New York's gallery owners, performers, and theater-company directors.

...

Newsmaker

Some Supreme Court justices are well known, others are somewhat low profile, yet no other has received as much media coverage as Ruth Bader Ginsburg. As the legend of the elderly feminist justice with a passion for dissenting grew during her later years, Ruth became a global human headline. The media tracked everything from her wardrobe choices to her health status very closely – making her the first justice of the Supreme Court of the United States to become a household name around the world.

O is also for

On the Basis of Sex

Released in 2018, *On the Basis of Sex* is an inspirational biopic that depicts Ruth's life as a new mother and young attorney navigating the legal system during a time when gender discrimination was rife. The movie was directed by Mimi Leder and written and produced by none other than Ruth's own nephew, Daniel Stiepleman.

...

Orator

Apart from being an incredible writer, Ruth also had the gift of the gab. From delivering concise legal arguments in courts to giving moving keynote speeches at graduation ceremonies, Ruth was known as a great orator, delivering speeches and addresses in a slow, thoughtful manner.

...

Oklahoma

While Ruth was born in New York and lived most of her life in Washington, DC, the girl from the north spent two years of her life, from 1954, living at Fort Sill, Oklahoma, the home of the US Army's Field Artillery – Marty, who was in the Army Reserve, was serving at Artillery Village. Ruth noted the discrimination black and First Nations people faced in the south. Later in life, Ruth would go on to advocate for marginalized communities facing discrimination.

...

Obergefell v. Hodges

On 26 June 2015, the Supreme Court of the United States ruled on *Obergefell v. Hodges* – a momentous case that gave same-sex couples the right to marry in the United States. Ruth's oral arguments during the historic case were instrumental in ensuring a 5–4 ruling in favor of legalizing marriage between same-sex couples, thus cementing Ruth's standing as a strong ally of LGBTQI+ people.

Following Ruth's death, opera houses around the US dimmed their lights to honor her passing.

Along with fellow Supreme Court justice Antonin Scalia, Ruth appeared as an extra in the Washington National Opera's 1994 production of Richard Strauss' *Ariadne auf Naxos* on its opening night.

During a guest spot on a Chicago radio show, Ruth named Mozart's *Marriage of Figaro* and *Don Giovanni* as her top two favorite operas, with Strauss' *Der Rosenkavalier*, Verdi's *Otello*, and Puccini's *La fanciulla del West* completing her list of her top five fave operas.

Two songs by legendary Italian opera composer Giacomo Puccini were performed at Ruth's private funeral, held at Arlington National Cemetery.

Ruth had many loves in her life: her family, her country, and the law. But opera also captured Ruth's heart early on in her life, and it never let go. Ruth's long love affair with the art form was ignited when she saw her first performance of Ponchielli's *La Gioconda* as an eleven-year-old. She carried this passion for opera throughout her life, attending performances around the world and listening to her favorite arias again and again. As an ardent opera fan and high-profile advocate of the arts, Ruth was well known to opera companies and institutions, which embraced her zeal for artistic performance so much that she was invited onstage frequently. In 2016 she got her big break: a speaking role playing the Duchess of Krakenthorp in a production of Donizetti's operatic rom-com *The Daughter of the Regiment* at Washington National Opera. Audiences went wild seeing Ruth perform. Becoming an opera star at 83 is proof that you're never too old to kick life goals.

O is for OPERA

P is for

POP CULTURE

The pop culture and Supreme Court scenes don't cross over often, yet as Justice Ruth Bader Ginsburg slowly morphed into the Notorious RBG, the pop culture world responded by honoring her with memes, merch, TV skits, talk-show appearances, and movie cameos. She was even the subject of a *Saturday Night Live* sketch, signaling her arrival as a public figure of note. Most famous people caricatured by *SNL* cross their fingers and hope the skits aren't cruel, but Ruth had nothing to worry about. Actor, writer and comedian Kate McKinnon famously impersonated Ruth for several *Saturday Night Live* skits, flinging spicy "Gins-burns" (geddit?) at opponents. The sketches caught the attention of Ruth herself, who said she'd too like to whip out the odd "Gins-burn!" to her adversaries.

Wearing her trademark decorative collar and wielding a teeny-tiny gavel, Ruth was immortalized in Lego form with a cameo appearance in *The Lego Movie 2: The Second Part*.

In 2019, *MTV* bestowed on Ruth the inaugural Best Real-Life Hero award.

From sweatshirts to candles and mugs, there's plenty of RBG-themed merch on the market, but perhaps one of the most inspired is the toaster that will burn Ruth's face into your bread so you can enjoy a slice of the Supreme Court justice for breakfast.

NOTORIOUS R.B.G

NOTORIOUS RBG

YOU CAN'T HANDLE THE RUTH

Historic footage of Ruth Bader Ginsburg featured in the video for "I'll Fight", a song performed by Oscar-winner Jennifer Hudson for the RBG documentary.

Comedic actor Pete Davidson got a Ruth Bader Ginsburg tattoo in 2018. After her passing, many more fans got inked with tributes to RBG.

P is also for

Presidents

Ruth met many US presidents during her time working in public service. She enjoyed a special relationship with Barack Obama, based on mutual admiration and respect, even though it was reported that she once left a White House dinner with Obama to work out with her personal trainer!

...

Parents

Born in 1933, Ruth was Nathan and Celia Bader's second daughter; her older sister, Marilyn, passed away when Ruth was a toddler. Her father was a quiet man who made a humble living as a merchant, while her mother, Celia, was an early feminist who encouraged her daughter to read, write, study, and find a career of her own instead of relying on a man for security.

...

Professor

With a mind as sharp as an axe and a love for the written word, it's unsurprising that Ruth was an excellent scholar. In 1963 (at the tender age of 30) Ruth was given an associate professorship at Rutgers Law School. Then, in 1972, she became the first tenured female faculty member at Columbia Law School – a truly historic achievement.

...

Pregnancy Discrimination Act

Ruth recognized pregnancy discrimination as a very real issue. In the 1970s she worked alongside other determined women to establish the Coalition to End Discrimination Against Pregnant Workers, which lobbied for – and succeeded in ending – pregnancy discrimination. In 1978, the *Pregnancy Discrimination Act* came into being, meaning any discrimination against pregnant women in the workplace from that point on was unlawful.

Q is also for

Queen

Although Ruth was once dubbed "The Queen of the Internet" and was often depicted wearing a crown, being Queen Ruth wasn't exactly appealing to her. Instead, she was quoted as saying, "I'd rather be notorious." In the end, she got her wish and will forever be known as Notorious RBG (even though she remains a queen to many).

...

Quest

Ruth's life resembled a real hero's journey. From her humble beginnings in Brooklyn to her ascension to the Supreme Court of the United States, the story of Ruth had a quest-like quality. She was presented with considerable hurdles (personal loss, gender discrimination, and cancer diagnoses, to name just a few of the challenges she faced), yet each obstacle on her path was swept aside on her quest for justice.

...

Martin-Quinn score

Devised by political scientists Kevin Quinn and Andrew Martin, the Martin-Quinn score rates US Supreme Court justices on a scale from liberal to conservative, based on their decisions. Positive scores denote conservative thinking while negative scores equate to more liberal ideology. Scores have been allocated for all Supreme Court justices who have served since October 1937. Unsurprisingly, during her final term, Ruth scored a -2.82, making her the second-most liberal justice on the Supreme Court bench for the year, just behind Justice Sonia Sotomayor on -3.48.

One of the final cases Ruth presided over during her 27-year Supreme Court stint was *Bostock v. Clayton County* in 2020. She voted with the majority to rule that discrimination against LGBTQI+ people within the workplace was illegal. The case came about after a long-term employee was fired soon after joining a gay softball league.

Ruth officiated at the wedding of Ralph Pellecchio and Dr James Carter Wernz, the first same-sex couple to get married at the Supreme Court. She even helped them to write their wedding vows.

When Ruth passed away, the official *RuPaul's Drag Race* Twitter account tweeted: "Ruth Bader Ginsburg inspired generations with her unwavering commitment to give every American the right to freedom and equality. Rest in Power, RBG."

is for QUEER RIGHTS

Although Ruth was primarily known as a defender of women's rights, her decisions while sitting on the bench of the US Supreme Court showed strong commitment to LGBTQI+ equality. Over the decades she joined key rulings that struck down anti-gay laws, with most of these rulings being incredibly close, 5–4 calls. One vote either way, and the US could have been a very different place for the queer community to live in. Most famously, in 2015 she joined the majority in *Obergefell v. Hodges*, a crucial case that struck down state bans on same-sex marriage, making full marriage equality a nationwide reality for Americans. She then went on to officiate at same-sex unions, fulfilling her duties as both an anti-discrimination advocate and a gay ally.

R is for REPRODUCTIVE RIGHTS

WE ARE NOT OVARY-ACTING

While women and their allies were fundraising and marching in the streets to protect the reproductive rights of women, Ruth repeatedly took on the cause in the courts. From her pivotal work with the ACLU Women's Rights Project in the 1970s to her time sitting on the bench of the Supreme Court, Ruth clocked up an impressive half a century of work championing reproductive rights. Whether it was ensuring safe, legal abortion access or fighting for women's right to access contraceptives under their employer's health insurance plans, Ruth led landmark legal cases and presided over many important decisions that impacted on women's reproductive rights in the US. Despite it being a polarizing, contentious topic, Ruth never took a step backwards from it, always defending the creeping encroachments on the right of women to determine their own fates and have agency over their bodies.

In the 1970s, the US Air Force changed its policy that required women to either resign or get an abortion after becoming pregnant. This change came about due to a lawsuit led by Ruth, who represented Captain Susan Struck, a woman who discovered she was pregnant while serving in Vietnam.

In 2020, Ruth issued a dissent relating to a case that sought to allow companies the right to refuse employees medical coverage for contraceptives. The ruling declared that it was acceptable for the government to allow companies to deny contraceptive coverage on religious grounds, but Ruth's strong dissent remains on the record.

A significant US Supreme Court win for abortion access occurred in 2016, when *Whole Woman's Health v. Hellerstedt* was seen before the Supreme Court. Justice Ginsburg and other justices ruled that some abortion restrictions in Texas were unconstitutional, paving the way for more women to receive access to safe, legal abortion in that state. In 2021, abortion rights were, controversially, once again rolled back in Texas, showing how precarious laws can be.

TEXAS

R *is also for*

Reed v. Reed

In 1971, Ruth's first case on behalf of the ACLU was heard before the US Supreme Court. Ruth was arguing *Reed v. Reed* – a case that sought to overturn an Idaho law that automatically gave men the authority to administer deceased estates. In this particular case, a woman was arguing for the right to administer her deceased son's estate. Ruth won the case, which represented both a significant win for gender equality and a real stepping stone for Ruth to go on to further advance women's rights cases in the courts.

...

Role model

On a one-on-one level, Ruth was an important role model to the law clerks and students she mentored as a professor and jurist. But more broadly, she was a role model to millions of people she didn't know who believed in the concept of justice for all, from young women hoping to study law when they grew up to grandmas attending women's marches around the world.

...

Rosh Hashanah

Ruth passed away at the beginning of Rosh Hashanah, also known as Jewish New Year. The timing of her death held great significance for the Jewish community, which believes that righteous people die just before the new year because their presence is needed until the very end of the year. Although the timing of Ruth's death was unfortunate from a political point of view, from a religious standpoint it was a particularly poignant time for her to pass away.

S is also for

Antonin Scalia

Ruth's long-standing friendship with fellow New Yorker, Justice Antonin Scalia, was a source of fascination for many. Despite holding opposing views on many legal and political matters, the two had an enduring friendship based on a mutual love of opera and the law. Ruth formed a friendship with Antonin while they served together on the US Court of Appeals for the District of Columbia Circuit in the 1980s. Their close bond continued until Antonin's death in 2016. The two vacationed together and celebrated New Year's Eve together with their families. Their friendship was even immortalized in *Scalia/Ginsburg*, a comedic opera composed by Derrick Wang.

...

Supreme Court

In 1993, Ruth was appointed to the Supreme Court of the United States by then president Bill Clinton. As only the second woman to become a Supreme Court justice, Ruth replaced Justice Byron White, who was a pro footballer before serving as a Supreme Court justice for 31 years.

...

Scrunchies

From accessorizing her judicial robes with elaborate collars to donning fine lace gloves like 1980s-era Madonna, Ruth emerged as a most unlikely fashion icon thanks to following her own fashion rules. When it came to hair accessories, the humble scrunchie was one of her mainstays. While the 90s accessory had a strong comeback in the late 2010s, Ruth was already onto a good thing, keeping her ponytail in place with a comfy scrunchie for decades before it became cool again. As a scrunchie connoisseur, Ruth even ranked cities for their scrunchie quality, with Zurich, London, and Rome among her top three places to shop for the hot, then not, then hot again ponytail holder.

Visionary politician Olof Palme became prime minister of Sweden in 1969. His views on liberating women from entrenched gender roles at home by not cutting men any slack on their domestic responsibilities were key to shaping Ruth's views on gender equality.

Ruth's time in Sweden was spent collaborating with scholar Anders Bruzelius on the book *Civil Procedure in Sweden* (1965). In 1969, both were conferred with honorary doctorates at Lund University.

In 2019, Ruth travelled back to Sweden to receive a jubilee honorary doctorate from Lund University, a rare award given to scholars who have been honorary doctors for 50 years.

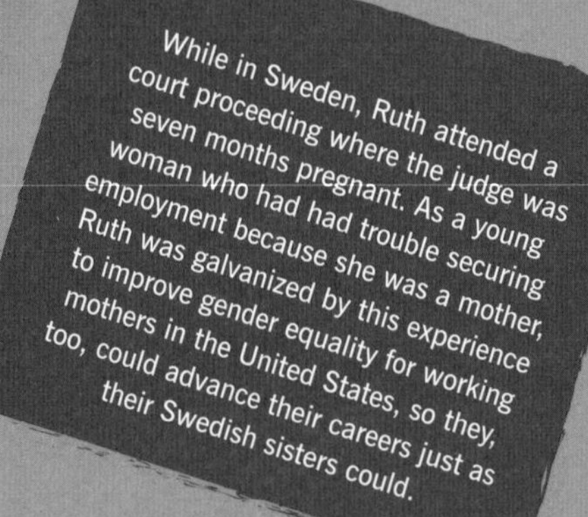

S *is for* SWEDEN

Scandinavia's reputation for being a beacon of progressive thought and policymaking isn't just hype – the region helped to shape the mind of a young Ruth Bader Ginsburg at a pivotal time in her life. In the early 1960s Ruth journeyed to Sweden to work on a legal research project at Lund University. Of course, true to her dedicated, scholarly nature, she had learned the Swedish language prior to traveling there. Ruth often said that her time in Sweden opened her eyes to gender equality – in Sweden, women represented a quarter of all law students, while only a tiny minority of American women studied law in the 1960s. Ruth also saw the positive impacts that flow from affordable childcare and the equal distribution of parenting duties between men and women. In the years after this trip, Ruth would work on groundbreaking gender discrimination cases.

T is for THEATER

While Ruth's first love was opera, she was fond of all the performing arts, including theater. A fixture of the New York and Washington, DC, theater scenes, Ruth was found in the audience of many opening- and closing-night performances. And just like her love of opera saw her gracing the stage in performances, multi-talented Ruth also took part in theater productions – proving that there isn't much this multi-tasking woman couldn't do! She participated in the Shakespeare Theatre Company's highly anticipated mock trials, so popular they sell out in minutes. She also joined other leaders in the Washington, DC, community to participate in *Our War*, a theatrical event about the US Civil War featuring monologues delivered by notable people. Ruth's theater cameos weren't just limited to the US, either – she also appeared as a judge (of course) in a performance of Shakespeare's *The Merchant of Venice*, held in Venice, Italy (of course).

Ruth was a big fan of *The Originalist*, a witty off-Broadway play about her friend and fellow Supreme Court justice Antonin Scalia. It was reported that Ruth saw the play multiple times.

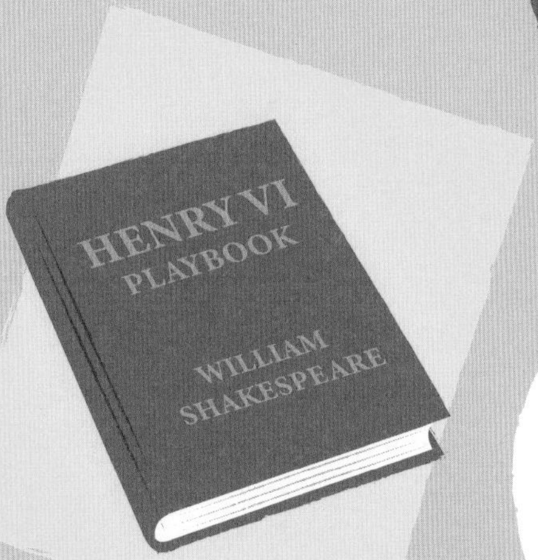

HENRY VI PLAYBOOK

WILLIAM SHAKESPEARE

Ruth appeared in a theater production of Shakespeare's *Henry VI*, delivering the famous line: "The first thing we do, let's kill all the lawyers," before adding her own line – "then the reporters."

When asked about her enduring love for the performing arts, Ruth replied that art "makes life beautiful."

T *is also for*

Trailblazer

Blazing a trail where few women had gone before was Ruth's calling. She was one of very few women to study at Harvard Law School at the time she was there. As only the second woman to sit on the US Supreme Court bench, Ruth showed the nation that having a woman as a Supreme Court Justice wasn't an anomaly. The cases she worked on while at the ACLU paved the way for women to stand up and demand equal rights and equal pay. As a trailblazer, it doesn't get much better than Ruth Bader Ginsburg.

...

***Time* magazine**

Getting your face on the front cover of *Time* magazine is a huge power move, and one that Ruth, of course, pulled off. She got the cover treatment in 1996 as part of the 100 Women of the Year project, then again in 2015, when she was named one of the 100 Most Influential People. In 2020 she appeared on a tribute cover following her death, wearing her signature jabot, gloves, and a knowing, wry smile.

...

Tzedek, tzedek, tirdof

Translating to "Justice, justice shall you pursue," these words from the Hebrew bible were proudly displayed in Ruth's chambers. This reminder of her commitment to ending injustice would guide Ruth through her days working on complicated and often controversial cases that came before the US Supreme Court during her 27 years of service.

U
is also for

Unconventional
Ruth's life was a masterclass in living life on your own terms. For a woman born in the US in 1933, studying and practicing law was a highly unconventional choice. Instead of marrying a man who expected her to give up her career to rear children, she partnered up with her beloved Marty, who not only supported her career aspirations, but delighted in donning an apron to assume the cooking duties. From her choice of partner to her decision to pursue a career in law at a time when women were expected to become homemakers, Ruth bucked the trends to live an unconventional life.

...

Underdogs
Some lawyers love nothing more than representing celebrities, while others chase cases that deliver huge paydays, but Ruth dedicated her legal career to representing underdogs. Unlike many in the legal field, her choice of profession wasn't driven by money, but a genuine interest in pursuing justice and ensuring that people who had been victims of inequality and discrimination had someone fighting in their corner.

...

Unwavering
If battling cancer several times wasn't enough, Ruth also stood tall and completed her duty to the court in the face of death threats from fringe groups. In a 2006 speech Ruth revealed that both herself and Justice Sandra Day O'Connor had received death threats, yet her approach to her work was unwavering. Despite being targeted with these threats, both Sandra and Ruth continued to show up to work to get the job done.

In 1999, Chih-Yuan Ho and Melissa Kay Graham became the first women to graduate from the Virginia Military Institute in its 160-year history. They both joined the school in 1997, following the landmark case that ruled that its all-male policy was unconstitutional.

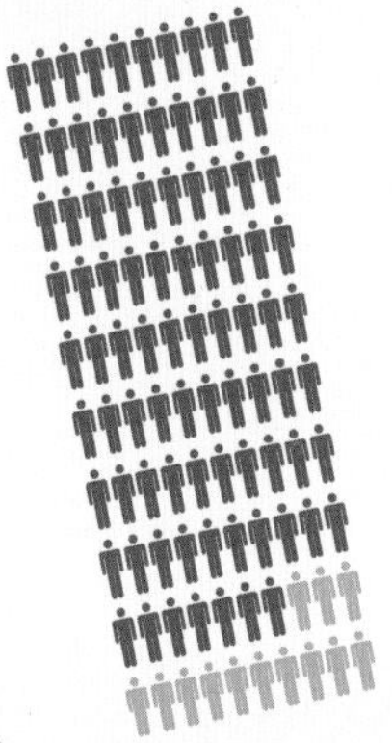

By 2019, women accounted for 13 per cent of cadets at the Virginia Military Institute.

As of 2021, 602 women in total have graduated from the Virginia Military Institute since 1997 – thanks to the landmark ruling handed down in 1996.

Many notable people have attended Virginia Military Institute, including beloved actor and comedian Mel Brooks, military figure General George S. Patton, and Virginia's governor, Ralph Northam.

U *is for* USA Vs VIRGINIA

For 160 years Lexington's Virginia Military Institute (VMI) only admitted male cadets. That was until Ruth wrote the majority opinion for the 1996 US Supreme Court ruling that ended the institution's male-only admission policy. Many people reacted negatively to the ruling, believing that women didn't have what it took to graduate from the tough school renowned for breaking people down. But Ruth held strong to her belief that women had much to offer the school, and she was right. Twenty-one years after she wrote that landmark majority opinion, Ruth visited the school and encountered the female cadets who lived and studied there. Since the ruling, women's presence and role in the military have grown and expanded, partly due to this important Supreme Court decision.

V is for VOTING RIGHTS

BALLOT BOX

Voter suppression has long been a hot topic in the United States, with many voting rights cases ending up in the US Supreme Court. It's unsurprising that Ruth was a staunch defender of voting rights. Perhaps one of the most interesting and prophetic cases Ruth presided over was *Shelby County v. Holder*. In 2013, a 5–4 ruling handed states greater power to remove preclearance, cut early voting opportunities, and close polling booths. These methods are often used strategically to make it difficult for minorities to vote – and Ruth was wise to this. Even though she was outnumbered in this case, she wrote a stinging dissenting opinion that made it very clear how the ruling was endangering democracy and leaving the door open to racist voter suppression. Since then, various states have introduced an alarming number of new laws that restrict access to the vote, with more expected to follow.

President Lyndon B. Johnson signed the *Voting Rights Act* on 6 August 1965, with civil rights heroes Martin Luther King Jr and Rosa Parks in attendance.

The *Voting Rights Act* of 1965 was introduced to prevent racial discrimination in voting, yet the 2013 *Shelby County v. Holder* case obliterated key parts of the Act that protected the voting rights of minorities.

In her final months, Ruth defended the constitutional rights of Wisconsin's citizens by writing a dissenting opinion against a controversial ruling that prohibited the extension of the absentee voting deadline in Wisconsin during the COVID-19 pandemic, which prevented many people from voting in person.

Ruth's dissenting opinion in the *Shelby County v. Holder* case includes the words: "Throwing out preclearance when it has worked and is continuing to work to stop discriminatory changes is like throwing away your umbrella in a rainstorm because you are not getting wet."

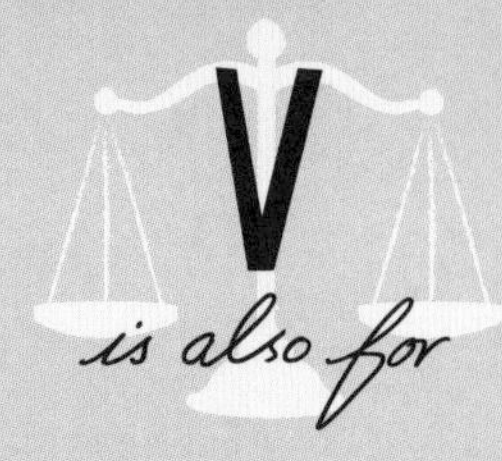

Vices

Even though she adopted epic workouts in her senior years, Ruth wasn't afraid to treat herself to good food and wine. She loved cracking open a bottle from California's Opus One winery to enjoy with other justices at the Supreme Court. And like a true New Yorker, she was partial to a poppy-seed bagel. When it came to desserts, her favorite was a frozen lime souffle made lovingly by her husband, Marty.

...

Vale

Ruth departed the earth on 18 September 2020 at the age of 87. While Ruth's funeral was a small, private affair, the public were able to honor her in other ways. As she lay in repose at the Supreme Court, thousands of people visited to pay their respects, stopping quietly by her casket, which was draped in the American flag. Afterwards, her coffin was moved to the US Capitol building for a service attended by her family, friends, and politicians. As the first woman and first Jewish American to lie in state at the US Capitol, Ruth ticked off a few more achievements, even in the afterlife.

...

Valiant

Meaning "to act with courage," valiant describes Ruth to a T. In the face of discrimination, she pushed forward to pursue a profession dominated by men. She took the discrimination cases she fought while working with the ACLU to the Supreme Court, and won many more battles than she lost. When it came to facing cancer, she valiantly fought on and continued to work while undergoing treatment. It takes great courage and determination to go against the grain and persist in the face of discrimination, inequality, and illness, and it's for this reason that Ruth earned the right to be called valiant.

W is also for

Work ethic

Ruth's work ethic was nothing short of epic. As a young mother she juggled caregiving while attending Harvard Law School, hitting the books after she'd put her daughter to bed. As a Supreme Court justice she was known for burning the midnight oil. The day after her husband Marty's death, Ruth returned to the Supreme Court bench, and only weeks after cancer surgery she returned to the court to fulfill her duties. Parenting, cancer treatment, and personal loss were just no match for Ruth's supreme work ethic.

...

Watergate

For 40 years, Ruth lived in an apartment in the famous Watergate complex, a series of residential buildings that are home to political power brokers, high-profile journalists, and other notable celebrities from the stage and screen. While the luxury complex has great appeal for anyone living in the public eye, its proximity to the Kennedy Center was also handy for opera-loving Ruth, who could easily dash over to watch Washington National Opera performances.

...

Weddings

Aside from upholding the Constitution, Supreme Court justices can perform marriage ceremonies, too. It's unsurprising that a hardworking woman like RBG would use her spare time to officiate weddings. Yep, RBG was big on the wedding circuit. In 2013, she made history by becoming the first Supreme Court justice to officiate at a same-sex wedding. Unstoppable in her commitment to help people get hitched, she even officiated a family friend's wedding only weeks before she died in 2020. True to form, even end-stage cancer couldn't stop Ruth from fulfilling her ceremonial duties.

Ruth moved to Washington, DC, in 1980 after then president Jimmy Carter appointed her to the United States Court of Appeals for the District of Columbia Circuit.

Ruth had a long-running connection with Washington, DC's Georgetown University Law Center. Her husband taught at the DC institution for years, but even after his passing, she'd return to the campus frequently to give talks to the law students and make surprise appearances in classes.

FIGHT LIKE RBG!

Thank You RBG

NOTORIOUS R.B.G

I DISSENT

The Supreme Court building was opened in Washington, DC, in 1935, 146 years after the Supreme Court itself was formed.

Washington, DC, is home to a hotel dedicated to female empowerment called Hotel Zena, which features a mural of Ruth Bader Ginsburg made from 20,000 hand-painted tampons. Yes, tampons.

ALL RISE

is for

WASHINGTON

Despite being a proud New Yorker, Ruth spent more than 40 years of her life living in Washington, DC, the nation's capital. For 27 years she served as a justice at the Supreme Court, an iconic DC building that became her second home. It's only fitting that someone who spent so long living and working in DC would become the first woman in history to lie in state at the US Capitol. Even in death, overachieving Ruth blazed another trail by also becoming the first Jewish American to lie in state at the US Capitol. Ruth loved Washington, DC, and the city's politically engaged residents loved her right back. After her death, residents held candlelight vigils on the steps of the Supreme Court and lined up in droves to pay their respects to their beloved judge. Her presence still lives on in the many RBG-themed murals that have been painted in DC.

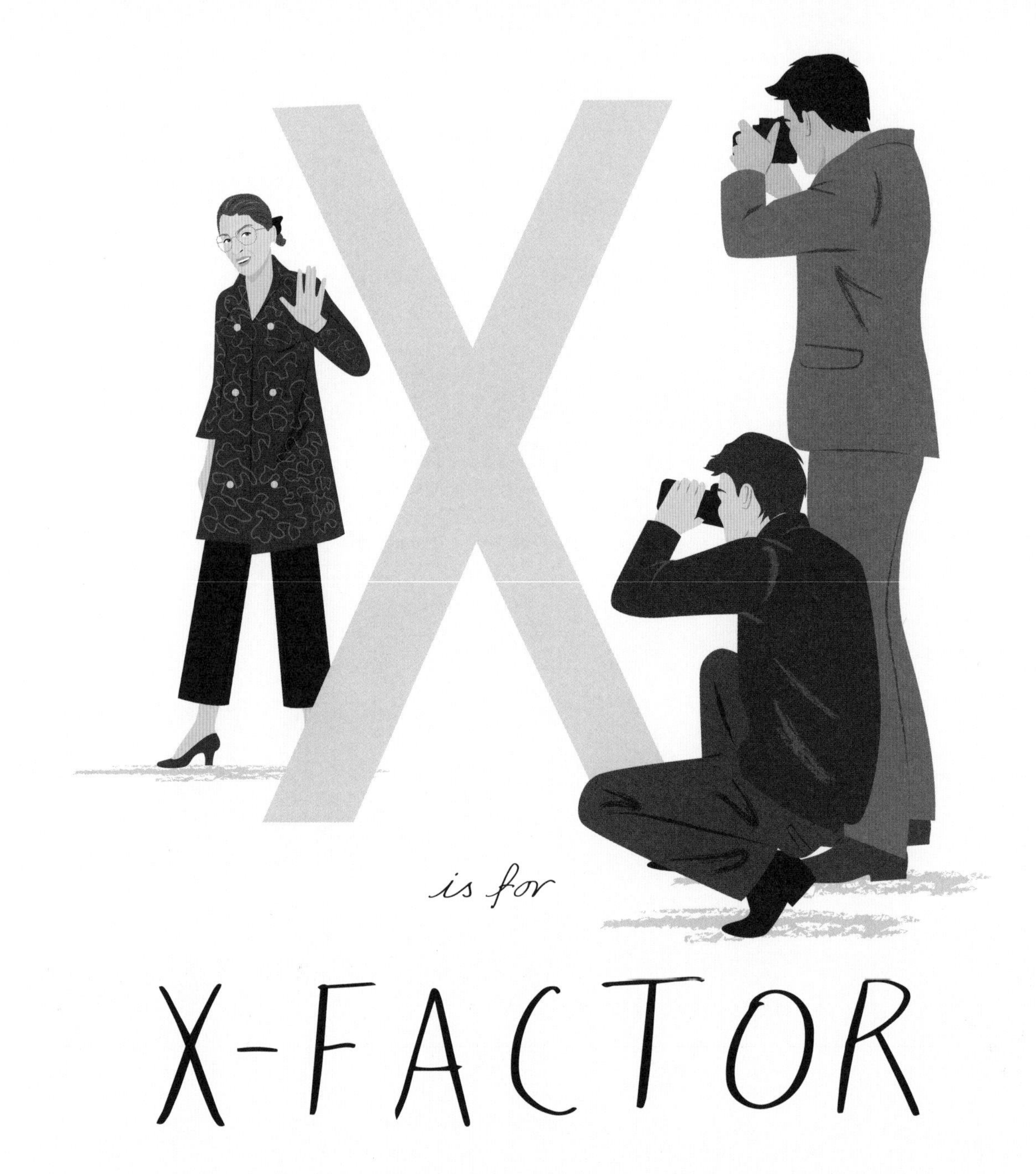

is for

X-FACTOR

US Supreme Court justices don't usually have big personalities that penetrate greater society, nor do they tend to become a one-woman cultural phenomenon. But in case you hadn't noticed, they broke the mould with Ruth. Unlike other justices, Ruth had the X-factor. From receiving a personal invitation from Jennifer Lopez to attend her show, to partying with popular *RuPaul's Drag Race* contestant Alexis Michelle, Ruth not only rubbed shoulders with celebrities, but was also treated like a celebrity herself. Never before had a Supreme Court justice enjoyed the limelight quite as much as Ruth. Celebrities and ordinary folk alike clamoured to meet and be photographed with her. What's most interesting about Ruth's X-factor is that it didn't come from being loud or bombastic – she managed to capture attention by being understated and considered in her speech. Ruth was extra without being extra.

When a stranger invited Ruth to attend her wedding, she responded with a thoughtful reply, stating she couldn't attend but was delighted to receive the "spirit-lifting" invite. Ruth's choice to not only RSVP but write a letter in return shows just how special she was.

X-ray
In 2018, fans were saddened to hear that Ruth was once again battling cancer after chest X-rays revealed cancerous nodules on her lungs. The X-rays were initially taken to monitor rib fractures she'd sustained the month before – injuries that didn't stop her from missing any oral arguments in court.

...

X-Force
Eagle-eyed viewers will notice that Ruth made a fleeting cameo appearance in Marvel superhero film *Deadpool 2*. Although she physically didn't act in the movie (like screen legends Brad Pitt and Matt Damon, who appeared briefly in the film), a headshot image of Ruth was shown during a scene when potential candidates for the X-Force strike team were being considered. Many considered Ruth to be a real-life superhero, so her appearance in a superhero movie was a clever nod to her standing.

...

Xmas
As a Jewish woman, Ruth noticed how Christian traditions were the accepted norm in the Supreme Court. "At Christmas around here, every door has a wreath," she said during an interview. Ruth "educated" the Supreme Court by displaying a mezuzah (a parchment scroll fixed to the door frames of Jewish homes) on the door of her chamber. She explained: "... it's a way of saying, 'This is my space, and please don't put a wreath on this door.'"

The media recognize X-factor when they see it. From being named *Glamour* magazine's Woman of the Year to appearing on *The Rachel Maddow Show*, *Late Night with Stephen Colbert*, *60 Minutes*, and other shows, Ruth and her whip-smart quips and never-say-die attitude helped her make a mark on the media.

While Ruth declined Jennifer Lopez's invite to attend her show (the concert start time was too late for the octogenarian to attend), Ruth invited JLo to her office in the Supreme Court, where Ruth shared some pearls of wisdom with the ageless pop star.

In an interview with *The New Republic*, Ruth said, "At my advanced age ... I'm constantly amazed by the number of people who want to take my picture."

Y *is also for*

Yom Kippur

As the holiest day of the Jewish calendar, Yom Kippur is hugely significant to the large number of Jewish people living in the US. When the US Supreme Court term was scheduled to start on Yom Kippur, Ruth successfully argued for the session to be rescheduled to the following day for the very first time. While moving a sitting may not appear like a big deal to an outsider, the traditions of the Supreme Court are rigidly adhered to and are rarely changed. Ruth's view was that allowing sittings to occur on Yom Kippur (or any other holy day) would be detrimental to both lawyers and judges.

....

Yellow

Ruth took dressing to match your mood to the next level when she started assigning specific decorative collars to her moves in court. In an interview with Katie Couric, Ruth divulged that she'd started wearing a special yellow crochet collar when announcing an opinion for the court.

...

Yiddish

Ruth's mother, Celia, grew up speaking the Yiddish language, but a generation later Ruth was speaking and writing in English as she grew up in the suburbs of Brooklyn. Many decades later, Ruth attended a performance of *Fiddler on the Roof* in Yiddish held in New York. More than half a century after her mother's passing, Ruth was watching a stage show performed in Celia's mother tongue.

Even though her yearbook indicates she played in the school orchestra, Ruth humbly admitted in later interviews that she played cello "not well."

Ruth's yearbook entry mentions she was a member of Arista, an elite honor society with strict criteria for entry.

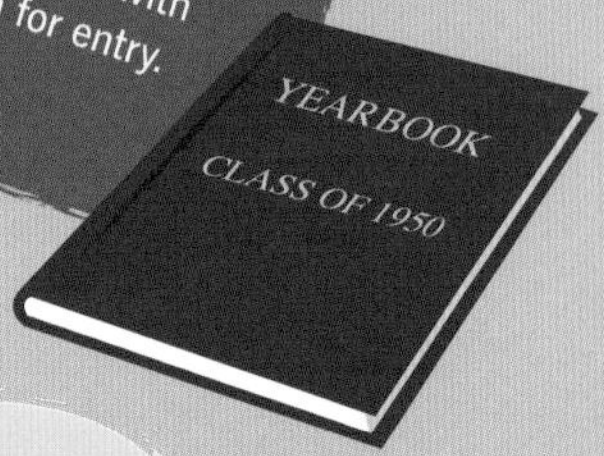

Ruth wrote many articles for her school newspaper, *The Highway Herald*. Her contributions to the newspaper included a mature and insightful article on the Magna Carta, indicating Ruth was somewhat destined to follow law as a career.

As a designated "Go-Getter," Ruth was tasked with encouraging people to support the high school's football and other sporting teams by attending big games.

Y *is for* YEARBOOK

Historians love digging through high-school yearbooks. Providing a portal to the past, a yearbook can be a great predictor of a person's future. Although Ruth's high-school yearbook didn't hint at her future as a judge, it did show she was a highly accomplished, industrious young woman with a bright future. Her yearbook entry indicates she was involved in a wide range of different activities and clubs, a quality she carried through her entire life. From baton twirling to playing cello in the school orchestra, serving as secretary to the English department chairman and acting as treasurer of the "Go-Getters" club, Ruth was a bona fide, well, go-getter. But wait, there's more! She's also listed as being a features editor of the school's term newspaper – a hint at great things to come for the legal eagle known for her sharp writing and editing skills.

People born between the mid 1990s and 2012 are loosely defined as belonging to Generation Z, and it's this group of youngsters who embraced the small-yet-mighty Supreme Court senior who championed inclusion and equality – and she embraced them right back. From wearing Ruth Bader Ginsburg costumes during Halloween celebrations to creating RBG-themed fan art, Gen-Z unofficially adopted Ruth as a folk hero. Ruth's accessibility and progressive views put her in good standing with young people, but it was what she stood for that undoubtedly sealed the deal with this generation. By helping to protect and enhance the rights of women, marginalized people, and the LGBTQI+ community, Ruth inspired a generation brought up in a world where inequality wasn't swept under the rug but put on the national agenda, where it belongs.

During an interview Ruth said that high-profile Gen-Z activists like Malala Yousafzai and Greta Thunberg gave her a sense of optimism about the future.

A year before she passed away, Ruth was quoted as saying that she found great hope in witnessing young people get "fired up" about the country.

Ruth loved sharing her knowledge with young people. For many years she was involved in the United States Senate Youth Program (USSYP), where she delivered keynote speeches and advice to the next generation of young leaders.

People who belong to Gen-Z are also known as "Zoomers." This hyper-connected generation are more likely to be politically engaged, tech-savvy and aware of global issues than all previous generations.

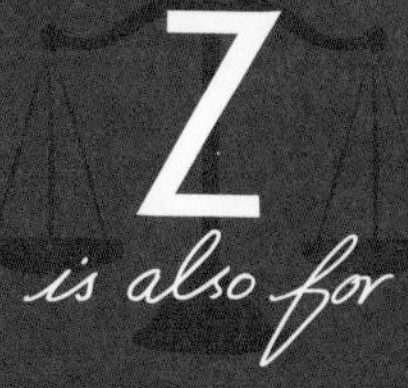

Z *is also for*

Zeitgeist

As Ruth's notoriety grew, she went from being relatively well known in legal circles to becoming a genuine cultural icon. But beyond being an icon, Ruth influenced the zeitgeist. Her rise to fame was driven by the cultural climate of the times – a time when more and more people were becoming interested in fighting inequality in all its forms. Ruth's body of work hit the big time at just the right time to contribute to the cultural zeitgeist.

...

Zenith

Very few of us can say we've reached the zenith of our careers, but Ruth belonged to a small club of greats who managed to reach the top of their career mountains. For a young mother to attend Harvard Law School in the 1950s was a monumental achievement, and to be appointed as a Supreme Court justice later in life was another. For a law scholar operating in the US, there is no greater honor than to be appointed to the Supreme Court, and Ruth not only got there, but managed to stay there for 27 highly productive (and influential) years.

...

Zzzz

In 2015, Ruth was famously caught sleeping in the chambers during then president Obama's State of the Union address. Earning kudos from anyone who has ever fit in a sneaky nap while on the job, Ruth admitted she wasn't "100 percent sober" during the speech, thanks to indulging in some fine wine during dinner beforehand.

Published in 2022 by Smith Street Books
Naarm | Melbourne | Australia
smithstreetbooks.com

ISBN: 978-1-92241-767-1

Publisher: Paul McNally
Project editor: Aisling Coughlan
Editor: Rowena Robertson
Design: Michelle Mackintosh
Illustrations: Chantel de Sousa
Proofreader: Pamela Dunne

Printed & bound in China by C&C Offset Printing Co., Ltd

Book 197
10 9 8 7 6 5 4 3 2 1

A
B
C
D
E
VOTES
FOR
WOMEN
EQUALITY
FOR
WOMEN
F
G
H
I
SUPER
DIVA
J
K
L
M